21 Days of Highs and Lows

AF624577

Carlos Catá Ruiz

BookLeaf Publishing

Presentation by *BookLeaf Publishing*

Web: www.bookleafpub.com

E-mail: info@bookleafpub.com

ISBN: 9789357442237

First edition 2023

1/21

These days
I write you poems in my head
I don't commit them to paper
I save them for rainy days
Hoping that you'll call
Longing to hear my voice
Missing the way my words
Stirred emotions in you
That you had never felt before
Just as your presence
Still does to me

2/21

I am not your ideal man
Not the husband you pictured
In your mind's eye
And I wish I could rewrite my past
But if I changed my past
Would fate had brought us together
As it has today?
Would the stars have aligned
They way they did on that starry night?
Would our paths have crossed
Forcing us into each other's lives
The way that it did?
There will be no answers
To these questions in this lifetime
I guess I'll just have to wait for the next

3/21

My heart sinks
As she tells me
All the reasons why
We can't be together
While in my heart
I see all the reasons
Why we should be

4/21

When the days are long
And the nights are cold
When the music has died
And your feet are tired of dancing
Will my warm embraces
And loving kisses
Be what you long for the most?

5/21

I remember you
As I walk by
That random pink decor
In the streets
or in the stores
Like that random
Pink door in the Keys
Or that pink Christmas gnome
on sale at Home Decor
I remember you
In the sour gummies
I crave to eat
And in every lyric
Of every song
That blares on the stereo
The memory of you
It's imprinted on my mind
And I cannot escape you

6/21

My mind has settled the matter before us
It's time to move on, I'm a big boy
Sometimes things in life don't pan out
As we thought they would
But my heart, he hasn't received the memo
He continues to hold on
Strung out on hope
He keeps me latched to the memories
Of your kisses, of your hand in mine
Of how I would get lost in your eyes
And how your smile brightened my days
So I'm stuck, like a tire in a ditch
I press on the throttle to move forward
But my tire, my heart, it digs in deeper
Refusing to let me go
Refusing to let me live and love anew
As I know I must do

7/21

I am in love with you
I cannot escape it
I can no longer deny it
I am in love with all that you are
Your ideals and your morals
In the way you carry yourself
Out in public and behind closed doors
You are the quintessential woman
I've searched for high and low

8/21

i'm down the street
from your house
and I think of the moments
we shared outside your home
how you'd meet me out front
your smile welcoming me in
minutes turning into hours
talking and laughing
sharing our life's stories
never could I have imagined
that it would come to an end
so I drive past
hoping to see you outside
that you'll wave for me to stop
to give me your smile
and tell me once again
that you see a future with me
instead all I see
is this lonely road
and broken dreams

9/21

I've lost all hope that someday
You and I will be as one
I know longer trust my instincts
No longer trust
the butterflies in my stomach
Or that keen sense of
Just knowing something is RIGHT
You felt right... feel right
In your eyes I saw everything
We would grow to be
But that we aren't
And never will…

10/21

I thought of you today
And your memory
Didn't stir that yearning
It usually does
Maybe it's because
I'm coming to terms
With the idea that
Loneliness is my new lover
That she is the one who
Greets me when I get home
Who lays next to me in bed
And strokes my head
Telling me
That I am enough

11/21

There's this underlying hypocrisy
in modern dating
we build profiles in apps
set parameters of what
our ideal matches should be
How their appearance needs to be
and what their likes should be
the options are countless
And yet...
when loves taps us on the shoulder
when Cupid draws his bow
and takes aim at our hearts
all the do's and don'ts amount to nothing
ALL those criterias we fooled ourselves
into believing we wanted become irrelevant
For love has no rhyme or reason
it has no parameters
Our souls simply know
when they've found that person
The one that makes them whole
For we were not made to be alone
Although we are born alone
and die alone
We were made to love
and to live in unison

We crave it as the trees crave
water and light
It is the driving force of life

12/21

Every night when I get home
I place the mask I wear for the world
On a hanger next to the door
It disguises the pain I feel in my heart
It has a smile plastered onto it
It tells the world that "I'm OK"
That I'm strong and learning to live
Without you
Love

13/21

Today, I am but a shell of a man
With no hope in sight
There is only this emptiness
A void that is vast and wide
A darkness that has enveloped me
And refuses to let me go
I am not angry
I am not in despair
The thought of ending my life
Is no longer a threat against
Those who've rejected or harmed me
It's an acceptance of my destiny
Of a life without meaning or worth
I willingly move towards it
Rejoicing in the peace it offers
Goodbye

14/21

I want you to choose me
As I choose you
Daily and without hesitation
This is true love
Where we stand united
Knowing that the dark days
Will surely come
But that our commitment
To each other
Is stronger than anything
That this world could ever throw at us

15/21

If I could have one wish granted
It would be for your soul
To remember mine
So that I don't have to wait
Another lifetime
Before we're reunited again

16/21

Thoughts of suicide
Circle my head
I don't want to die
Not any more
Not after meeting you
And falling in love with
The possibilities of a life
That could be
But having loneliness
As my lover now and not you
Well it's almost more than I can bear
The coldness of her touch
Compared to your smile alone
Is enough to drive me mad
The coziness of our space
Now suffocates me
And I surrender myself
To the darkness
Of being alone
Without you

17/21

I don't think of you
As often as I used to
And I can let time pass
Between our texts
Without it driving me crazy
However
When you post a picture
On Instagram
I have to fight the urge
To tell you just how radiant you are
That you are the single most
Beautiful girl on this planet
And that my heart
It still belongs to you

18/21

I use the colors you left behind
Spread them thin around
The canvas of my life
Adding water to make them last
The edges fading into nothing
I'm just trying to keep them
From colliding and mixing
Becoming nothing more than
A solid color of black
Like a cover-up tattoo
That was never meant to be
Imprinted on my skin
Or into my soul
I want to keep the hope it provided
Regardless if you're here or not

19/21

I want you to yearn for me
The same way trees crave the sun
How when battered and toppled over
They lean in and grow towards the light
Nothing keeps them from it
They twist themselves if need be
Just to be in its presence
That's how I want you to want me
To know that nothing could keep
You from being with me
Because that's how I want you

20/21

I fell in love with you
Like a tsunami attacks the shore
I was fierce and I didn't hold back
My intention was to break all barriers
Leave no room for misinterpretation
Love you like no one ever had
Or ever could again
At first you welcomed me
You let my tides roll in
Floated on the waters smiling
You loved how deep and vast
My feelings were for you
But the abyss that lied beneath
The reality of that depth
Did it scare you?
When did the water recede?
Was it you that doubted
Your ability to withstand the current
Or was it someone else?

21/21

The truth is that I love you
That I pretend to be moving on
When all I really want
Is for you to call me
Tell me that you miss me
That you've been struggling
With not having me near you
The you miss the sound of my voice
The softness of my lips against yours
The warmth of how I treated you
So I look for you in other Angels
I hope their wings can envelope me
Shield my eyes from seeing you
Distract me long enough
To imagine that maybe
You were just a dream
And that love
It isn't meant to feel so good

www.ingramcontent.com/pod-product-compliance
Lightning Source LLC
Chambersburg PA
CBHW051720130826
49812CB00034B/1279
9789357442237